Created, published, and distributed by Knock Knock
1635 Electric Avenue
Venice, CA 90291
knockknockstuff.com

Illustrations by Gemma Correll

This book is a work of editorial nonfiction meant solely for
entertainment purposes. It is not intended to create
actual panic or serve as psychological advice or counsel.
In no event will Knock Knock be liable to any reader for
any damages, including direct, indirect, incidental, special,
consequential, or punitive damages, arising out of or in
connection with the use of the information contained in
this book. So there.

Every reasonable attempt has been made to identify
owners of copyright. Errors or omissions will be corrected
in subsequent editions.

ISBN: 978-168349004-3
UPC: 825703-50138-4

10 9 8 7 6 5 4 3 2 1

100
Reasons
to Panic®
about
Doing Yoga

KNOCK KNOCK®
VENICE, CALIFORNIA

1.

Yoga will be booooooring.*

*Isn't it nice not to look at your phone for an hour or more?

2.

Everyone in class can do headstand— except you.*

*Yet you're still doing yoga.

3.

You won't know any of the asana names.*

*That's what beginner classes are for.

4.

You'll fall asleep during savasana.*

*Who couldn't use a few more Zzz's?

5.

You're a dude— you're not bendy enough.*

*All the more reason to take a class.

6.

You're just not bendy. Like, at all.*

*Hey, you know what might help? Yoga.

7.

Your instructor will use you as an example—of how not to do a pose.*

*She noticed you!

8.

Yoga mats and props will overtake your life—and your living room.*

*All that squishy material will make your house safe for impromptu toddler parties.

9.

Chanting? Really?*

*According to some research,
it lowers blood pressure.

10.

It's going to be hard.*

*Well, if it doesn't kill you,
it will make you stronger-ish.

11.

You won't really understand what "heart-opening" means.*

*Hint: it has nothing to do with cardiology.

12.

Clearing your mind is easier said than done.*

*Another point for meditation!

13.

Your precious vacation days will be spent at yoga retreats.*

*Time off that's actually relaxing? How novel!

14.

Yoga, yoga, yoga: do you talk about anything else?*

*What about yoga?

15.

You'll keep trying to do things more mindfully.*

*If calling laundry "mindful laundry" gets it done...

16.

Your attempts to be more spiritual will have you considering a move to an ashram.*

*Think of the quiet!

17.

You'll start a yoga blog.*

*You won't have to bore anyone
with your yoga stories.

18.

"My chakras are
out of alignment"
is your new "no."*

*It's more mysterious than
"I have to wash my hair."

19.

You'll develop a crush on your yoga instructor.*

*It's great motivation to keep going to class.

20.

Practicing yoga
at home will
reveal all the dust
bunnies under
your sofa.*

*Your floors are gonna be so clean!

21.

Every story you tell will start, "That reminds me of something my yoga teacher said..."*

*You're now a member of a select (albeit annoying) club.

22.

You're too old.*

*Better late than never.

23.

Now you say "Namaste" in farewell.*

*Perfect preparation for your pilgrimage to India.

24.

Goodbye, real clothing. Hello, yoga pants.*

*You'll be one of the few people actually wearing yoga pants for their intended purpose.

25.

Running burns more calories.*

*Running also means you have to wear shoes.

26.

You'll start daydreaming of quitting your job to do yoga teacher training.*

*Eventually, you'll get paid to do yoga!

27.

Focusing on your breath sounds easy but is actually hard.*

*Isn't that why you're practicing yoga—to work on that?

28.

You'll compare yourself to other yogis.*

*Isn't that why you're practicing yoga—to let go of those things?

29.

You'll try to get all your friends into yoga.*

*And then you can have yoga parties. Fun!

30.

You'll start talking in a yogic voice.*

---

*You'll be able to make annoying DMV lines get really chill, really quickly.

31.

You'll struggle with the Sanskrit.*

*You've always wanted to be a polyglot.

32.

"Yoga practice" sounds so highfalutin'.*

---

*Maybe you'll inpire others to refer to their "spinning practice" or "boxing practice."

33.

Straps, blocks, and other props are the only way you can get comfortable.*

*Don't you miss playing with blocks?

You have an attachment to a specific spot in the room for your mat.*

*You're like a regular at a corner bar—but with yoga.

35.

Standing in line at the grocery store will turn into a yoga session.*

*Better that than snapping at people for bringing too many items into the express lane.

36.

Your yoga mat goes everywhere with you.*

*It's less yappy than a small dog.

37.

You'll get into tantric sex.*

*Your online dating profile will really stand out.

38.

Your next trip to a tattoo parlor will end with a lower-back lotus tattoo.*

*It'll look so good in your yoga selfies.

39.

You don't have the right clothes for yoga.*

*Are you comfortable? You can do yoga.

40.

All your new yoga friends will want to eat macrobiotically, and you'll just want a hamburger.*

*They can do amazing things with adzuki beans these days.

41.

You'll decorate with statues of gods and goddesses.*

*No one will ever wonder what to get you for your birthday again.

42.

You'll find a guru.*

*Sounds cooler than a life coach or therapist!

43.

You won't find a guru.*

*It's the journey, not the destination.

44.

Dirty yoga mat
smells: yikes.*

*Finally, something to do with all that incense.

45.

Hot yoga will make you feel woozy.*

*Cheaper than a vacation
in the rainforest, though.

46.

You'll injure yourself.*

*You'll get to tell people you have a yoga injury.

47.

Your grandma will think you've joined a cult.*

*Maybe you can take her to yoga for seniors.

48.

You'll read cheesy self-help books, hoping to "figure yourself out."*

*Who said you have to solve your own mystery?

49.

Something will make you laugh— and you won't be able to stop.*

*You're "experiencing a release."

50.

Something will make you cry— and you won't be able to stop.*

*You're "experiencing a release."

51.

All that time looking at feet has you grossed out by them.*

*Perfect excuse to get a fresh pedicure.

52.

You'll talk yourself out of going when you're tired.*

*Sounds like it's time for yoga nidra—literally the "sleep of the yogis."

53.

Today, yoga. Tomorrow, juice cleanses.*

*Or tomorrow, a double espresso—
yoga doesn't judge!

54.

Your social life will vanish because you'll be too busy with yoga classes.*

*You'll make yoga friends.

55.

You'll have to give up your involvement in extreme sports.*

*Or you'll figure out a way to do yoga while skydiving.

56.

If you're a guy, you'll grow a scraggly beard.*

*You can braid it for extra flair.

57.

You won't be able to find a meditation cushion that matches your decor.*

*Voilà, new business idea!

58.

Everyone around you will make lots of "ahhhhhh" or "mmmmm" noises.*

*Not everyone gets to experience a human white noise machine.

59.

New-agey music is the only music you listen to now.*

*When people get in your car,
they'll immediately mellow.

60.

Your significant other will mock your yoga obsession.*

*Fine, you can do partner yoga
with someone else.

61.

Your coworkers will think you're weird with all that yoga.*

*Wait until they join you for lunchtime yoga.

62.

You'll keep falling over when you try to get into handstand.*

*Bruises and scrapes will make you look tough.

63.

Green juice is your new favorite drink.*

*Finally, you're getting the recommended daily allowance of fruits and vegetables.

64.

A perfect night in now means yoga and chanting.*

65.

Your breathing will get loud and weird.*

*Your Darth Vader impression
will be so realistic.

66.

You'll never master full lotus.*

*But you might master its seldom-known sister poses, "I'm in Agony Attempting Full Lotus" or "Baby Lotus."

67.

You'll skip happy hour for yoga class.*

*Your liver will thank you.

68.

You'll need another job to afford all those yoga classes.*

*You can get one at a yoga studio—surely you'd get a discount on classes, right?

69.

Scorpion pose— aka vrschikasana— makes you look ridiculous.*

*Aren't you supposed to be practicing non-judgment?

70.

You're too big
for yoga.*

*Yoga is for everybody (and every body).

71.

You're too petite for yoga.*

*Yoga is for everybody (and every body).

72.

You'll put an "om" sticker on your car.*

*You'll be able to distinguish your hybrid from all the other ones in parking lots.

73.

You won't be able to relate to your non-yoga friends anymore.*

*They're probably bitter and inflexible.

74.

You'll constantly be offering yoga as a cure-all for everything.*

*As long as you're not also
selling vitamins, you're good.

75.

You'll turn casual conversations into really deep ones.*

*You won't have to make small talk about the weather again.

76.

what if you're too inflexible?*

*Isn't that why you're doing yoga?

77.

what if you're too flexible?*

*Think of how fun you'll be at parties.

78.

You'll neglect your friends for yoga.*

*Maybe it's time to drag them to yoga with you.

79.

You'll neglect your partner for yoga.*

*Maybe it's time to drag
your sweetie to yoga with you.

80.

one day in class, you'll look up and start ranking butts.*

*You probably need to focus on your breath.

81.

You'll trade in coffee for sun salutations.*

*Slow down—yoga teachers have to get up somehow for those early classes.

82.

Finding the right yoga mat will be difficult.*

*It's like love—sometimes it finds you.

83.

You'll embrace
navel-gazing—
literally.*

*Your spine must be getting so flexible!

84.

You can't commit to a style of yoga, teacher, or studio.*

*You're committing to a yoga pu-pu platter.

85.

Your new dream: moving to a yurt.*

*Maintenance costs are significantly cheaper.

86.

You'll start to like the smell of patchouli.*

*Having a signature scent is a strong indicator of personal style.

87.

You'll spout inspirational, self-helpy sayings.*

*You'll be everyone's go-to for pep talks.

88.

You'll get into making vision boards.*

89.

You won't be able to relate to non-yogis.*

*They're probably boring.

90.

when you take a harder than usual class, you'll be really sore.*

*Guess you'll have to "nama-stay" in bed.

91.

When you can't make it to your favorite class, you'll be frustrated.*

*You'll be at the forefront of streaming classes.

92.

You'll do partner yoga—with your cat.*

*She'll love cat pose.

93.

You'll change your name from Sarah to something like Shanti.*

*People probably won't forget your name.

94.

Trying out new yoga studios is terrifying.*

*They're also ripe with possibility.

95.

You'll overdo it.*

*That's what child's pose is for.

96.

Mantras, auras, third eyes—whoa, that's a lot of woo-woo.*

*It'll make things less boring.

97.

Hot yoga classes mean potential skimpy-wardrobe malfunctions.*

*The room will be so steamy and sweaty that no one will notice.

98.

What if you fart during downward dog?*

*Most yogis don't know the Sanskrit for "Who farted?" so there's that.

99.

You'll want
to renounce
your worldly
possessions.*

*You won't have to hire a moving truck
next time your lease is up.

100.

You're too neurotic to achieve spiritual enlightenment.*

*Doesn't mean you can't try.

Don't worry. Just say "om."